Turtles of the Sea

by Clyde Hathers

SCHOOL PUBLISHERS

Cover, ©age fotostock/SuperStock; 3, ©Peter Cade/Iconica/Getty Images; 4, ©George Grall/National Geographic/Getty Images; 5, ©Lou Krasky/AP Images; 6, ©Carol Hughes/Bruce Coleman; 7, ©Earl Nottingham/Texas Parks and Wildlife Dept./AP Images; 8, ©Creatas/SuperStock; 9, ©Luiz C. Marigo/Peter Arnold, Inc.; 10, ©Doug Perrine/Peter Arnold, Inc.; 11, ©Brandon Cole/Visuals Unlimited; 12, ©Masa Ushioda/Visuals Unlimited; 13, ©age fotostock/SuperStock.

Copyright © by Harcourt, Inc.

All rights reserved. No part of this publication may be reproduced or transmitted in any form or by any means, electronic or mechanical, including photocopy, recording, or any information storage and retrieval system, without permission in writing from the publisher.

Requests for permission to make copies of any part of the work should be addressed to School Permissions and Copyrights, Harcourt, Inc., 6277 Sea Harbor Drive, Orlando, Florida 32887–6777. Fax: 407-345-2418.

HARCOURT and the Harcourt Logo are trademarks of Harcourt, Inc., registered in the United States of America and/or other jurisdictions.

Printed in Mexico

ISBN 10: 0-15-350291-6
ISBN 13: 978-0-15-350291-0

Ordering Options
ISBN 10: 0-15-349940-0 (Grade 5 ELL Collection)
ISBN 13: 978-0-15-349940-1 (Grade 5 ELL Collection)
ISBN 10: 0-15-357329-5 (package of 5)
ISBN 13: 978-0-15-357329-3 (package of 5)

> If you have received these materials as examination copies free of charge, Harcourt School Publishers retains title to the materials and they may not be resold. Resale of examination copies is strictly prohibited and is illegal.

> Possession of this publication in print format does not entitle users to convert this publication, or any portion of it, into electronic format.

2 3 4 5 6 7 8 9 10   126   12 11 10 09 08 07

Over the years, the number of different types of animals in the world has become smaller. Many species of animals have become endangered. An *endangered species* is a species that is close to becoming extinct. *Extinction* means that there are no more of a species left on the earth. A species can never come back once it is gone. The more we learn about endangered species, the more we can help animals survive.

Ridley Sea Turtle

Have you ever been to an aquarium or zoo? If you have, you have probably seen giant turtles swimming. Some of the turtles are very big. You might be tempted to jump on their backs and go for a ride.

The ridley sea turtle is in the same family as those giants. However, the ridley sea turtle is not quite as large. It is also close to extinction. There are two types of ridley sea turtles. One is called the olive ridley. The other is called the Kemp's ridley.

The Kemp's ridley is the smallest member of the sea turtle family. The Kemp's ridley turtle is usually 51 to 71 centimeters long, which is only about two feet long. These turtles have a shell that looks like a big gray heart. This makes identifying these turtles easier. The Kemp's ridley has a yellow belly like most turtles.

Kemp's ridleys lay eggs like all other turtles. Females usually lay their eggs between the months of April and August. The female turtles lay their eggs in groups of about a hundred. A female will lay eggs one to three times every nesting season. This means a Kemp's ridley turtle may lay over 300 eggs a year!

Once the eggs hatch, the baby turtles head for the ocean for their first meal of seaweed. Kemp's ridley turtles are not very picky about what they eat. Their diet is made up of anything smaller than themselves that lives in the ocean. The turtles will feed on crabs, fish, jellyfish, squid, snails, clams, starfish, and plantlife.

Kemp's ridley turtles can live for as long as twenty years when raised by humans. No one really knows their life span in the wild. However, one thing is certain, Kemp's ridleys are in danger.

Kemp's ridleys are the most likely of all sea turtles to become extinct. Human behavior is the main cause. Humans are destroying these turtles' habitat by polluting beaches and building homes on the coast. The females have trouble nesting. Many of the babies drown. They get caught in nets people use to fish. Every year, fewer and fewer eggs are laid.

The Kemp's ridleys are small turtles. However, they play a large role in the marine ecosystem. It is important to protect them so that they can increase their numbers.

Loggerhead Sea Turtles

Loggerhead sea turtles are enormous animals. They are about 3 feet (91.4 cm) long. They can weigh over 300 pounds (135 kg)! Their color is reddish-brown. The loggerhead sea turtle's block-shaped head gives it a different look. It has two sets of plates on top of its head that no other turtle has. You would not have any trouble identifying this giant if you were to see one.

Like many turtles, a loggerhead eats many different foods. It eats jellyfish, lobsters, shellfish, fish, and crabs. A loggerhead has hard jaws that help the turtle eat shellfish. Loggerheads also swim very fast. Catching food is never a problem for them. These turtles use their flippers to swim as fast as 25 miles (40.2 km) per hour.

Loggerhead turtles prefer warmer water when they nest. The coast of Florida and the Caribbean Sea are two of their favorite areas for laying eggs. Female loggerhead turtles can lay eggs up to seven times in one season.

The females can lay over a hundred eggs each time they nest. That means that one female loggerhead may lay over 700 eggs in one year! Loggerheads always return to the same spot to lay their eggs. Most sea turtles do this.

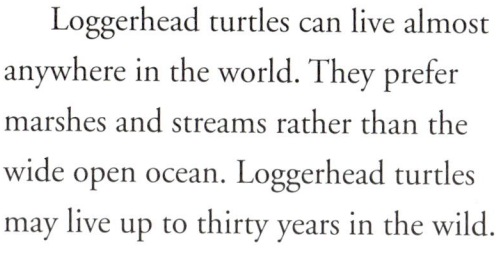

Loggerhead turtles can live almost anywhere in the world. They prefer marshes and streams rather than the wide open ocean. Loggerhead turtles may live up to thirty years in the wild.

If a loggerhead turtle is raised by humans, it could live to be fifty years old. That is a long time!

The population of loggerhead turtles has gone down in recent years. One reason is that the loggerheads get caught in shrimp and fish nets. Pollution is another main reason for the lower number of turtles. Luckily, loggerheads are not yet listed as endangered. Right now they are listed just as a *threatened species.* This means that they are close to being endangered. However, their population is safe from extinction for now.

It is not surprising that these turtles are slowly disappearing because of the problems turtles face. People who want to save the turtles try to help them in different ways. These people give out information about the animals. People try to make and change laws that will help the turtles. People also try to protect the turtles' environment. The hope is that with people's help, the number of turtles left on earth will keep growing.

Scaffolded Language Development

TENSE PRACTICE Remind students that the tense of a verb tells the time of the action. A *past tense* verb shows action that has already happened. Most past tense verbs use the ending *–ed* or *–d*. A verb in the *future tense* shows an action that will happen. To form the *future tense*, use the helping verb *will* before the main verb.

Have students read each of the following sentences three times: the first time as it is written in the present tense; the second time, changing the verb to the past tense; and the third time, changing the verb to the future tense. You may wish to use the first sentence as a model for students.

1. Kemp's Ridleys lay eggs like any other turtles.

2. We protect the turtles.

3. They prefer marshes and streams.

 Science

List and Respond Have students use an encyclopedia or the Internet to make a list of other endangered animals. Ask them to choose one animal and list the reasons the animal has become endangered and how the animal could be helped.

School-Home Connection

Endangered Animals Have students discuss with family members what they have learned about endangered animals. Then have them talk about how they might be able to help endangered animals.

Word Count: 872